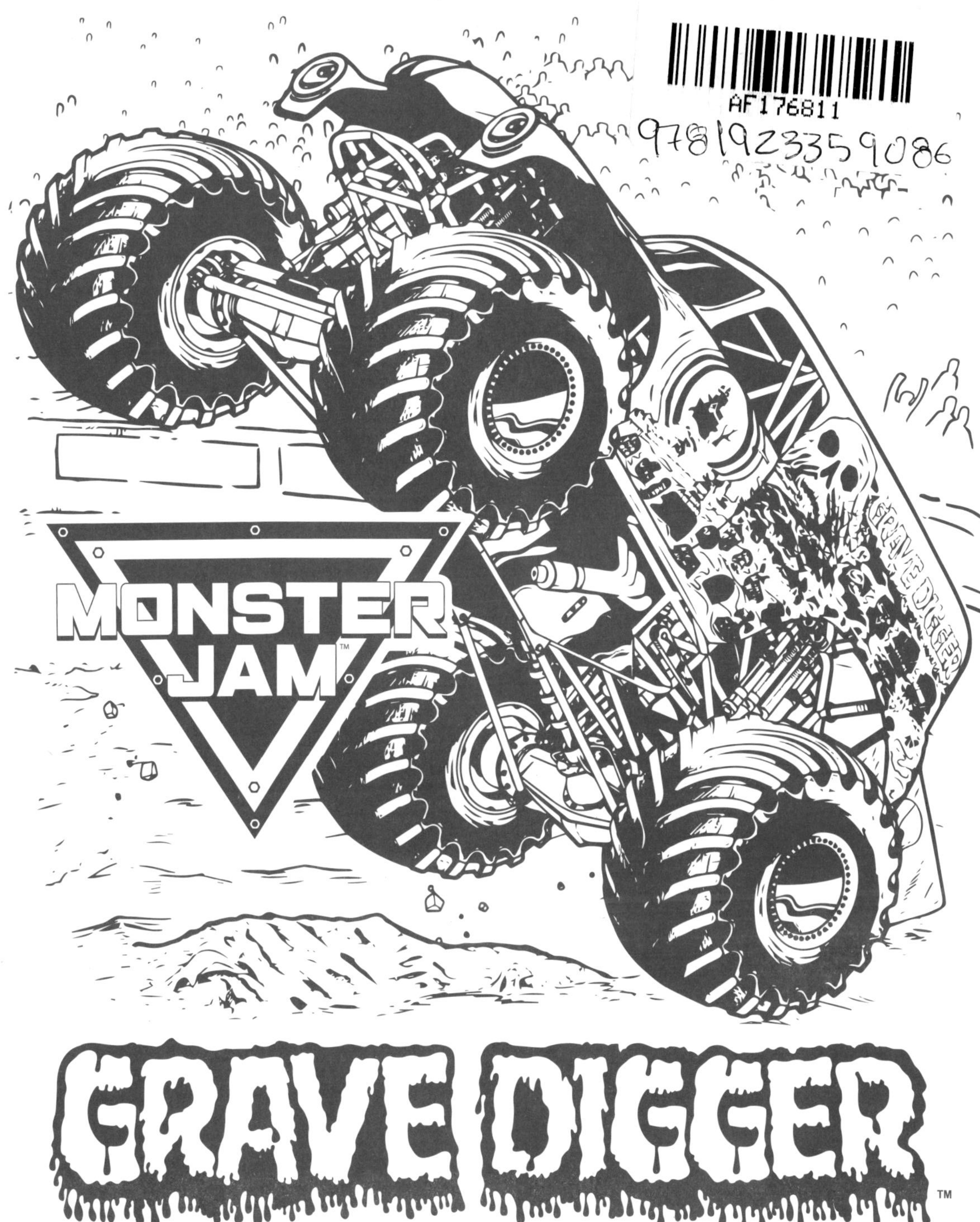


GRAVE DIGGER™

GRAVE DIGGER
ZOMBIE

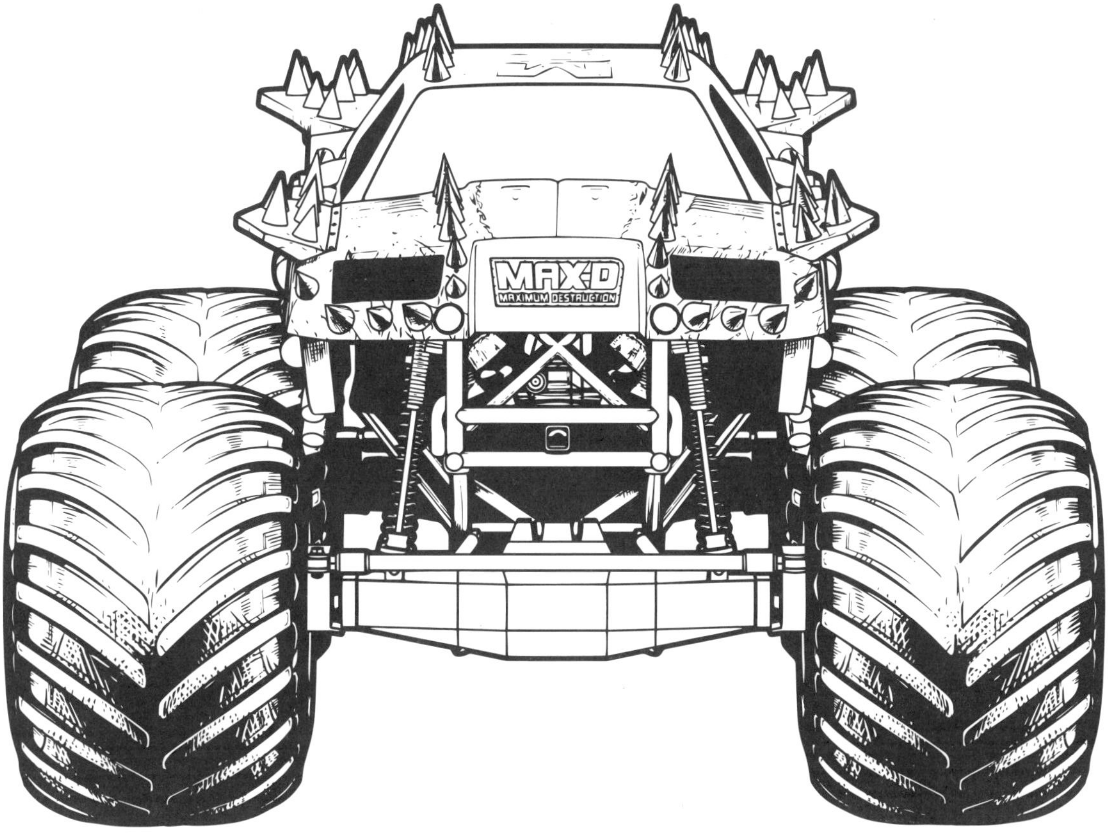

MAX-D
MAXIMUM DESTRUCTION
TM

MONSTER JAM™

Sparkle
SMASH™
Sparkle SMASH

Megalodon
El Toro Loco

ThunderRoarus™

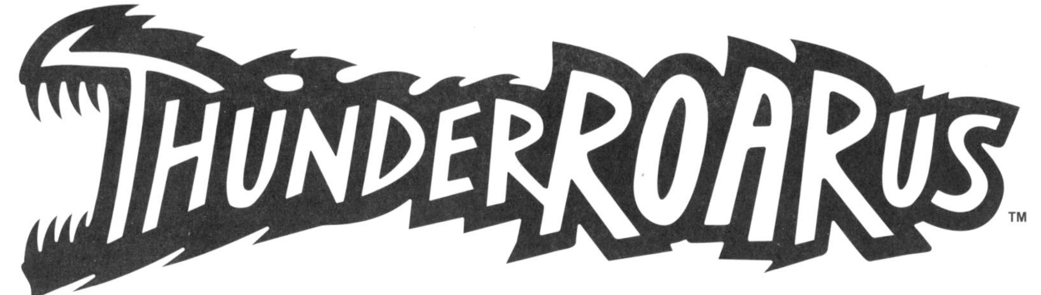

Monster Jam™

Pirate's Curse™

Zombie™

Monster Mutt™

MONSTER JAM
MEGALODON
MEGALODON
TM

MONSTER
JAM™

MONSTER
JAM™

Pirate's Curse
MONSTER JAM
Pirate's
Curse
TM

MAX-D
TOM MEENTS
MONSTER
JAM™

MONSTER
JAM
TM
GEAR
IT UP

THUNDERROARUS
™

El Toro
Loco™

MONSTER
JAM™

ZOMBIE
ZOMBIE
TM

MONSTER JAM™

Sparkle SMASH™

El Toro Loco™

MAX-D
MAXIMUM DESTRUCTION™

MEGALODON™

Sparkle SMASH
Sparkle SMASH™

MAX-D
MAXIMUM DESTRUCTION
™

Sparkle SMASH
MEGALODON
MAX-D
MAXIMUM DESTRUCTION

El Toro Loco™
El Toro Loco
MONSTER JAM
MONSTER JAM™

# GRAVE DIGGER™